EARLY AMERICAN FAMILY

Meet the Wards

on the Oregon Trail

by John J. Loeper

BENCHMARK BOOKS

MARSHALL CAVENDISH
NEW YORK

Benchmark Books
Marshall Cavendish Corporation
99 White Plains Road
Tarrytown, New York 10591-9001

Illustrations by James Watling
Musical score and arrangement by Jerry Silverman
Map by Rodica Prato
Photo research by Ellen Barrett Dudley

The photographs in this book are used by permission and through the courtesy
of: *The Image Bank:* Harald Sund, 10; *U. S. D. I. Bureau of Land Management,
National Historic Oregon Trail Interpretive Center, Baker City,* Oregon: 15, 16, 19,
22, back cover. *Breslich and Foss Limited:* 21. *Corbis-Bettmann:* 25. *Jeff Vanuga:* 37.
Eliot Cohen: 38, 58. *Scotts Bluff National Monument:* 40-41, 44-45, 91.

Library of Congress Cataloging-in-Publication Data
Loeper, John J. Meet the Wards on the Oregon trail / John J. Loeper.
p. cm.—(Early American family)
Includes bibliographical references and index.
Summary: Recounts the adventures of the Ward family, who traveled by covered
wagon from Missouri to California along the Oregon Trail in 1853.
ISBN 0-7614-0844-4 (lib. bdg.)
1. Pioneers—West (U. S.)—Social life and customs—Juvenile literature. 2.
Pioneers—West (U. S.)—Biography—Juvenile literature. 3. Frontier and pioneer
life—West (U. S.)—Juvenile literature. 4. Oregon Trail—Juvenile literature. 5.
West (U. S.)—Social life and customs—Juvenile literature. 6. Overland journeys
to the Pacific—Juvenile literature. 7. Ward family—Juvenile literature. 8. West
(U. S.)—Social life and customs. [1. Ward family. 2. Pioneers. 3. Frontier and
pioneer life—West (U. S.) 4. Oregon Trail.] I. Title. II. Series: Loeper, John J.
Early American family.
F593.L82 1999 978—DC21 97-42199 CIP AC
1999   CIP   AC

Printed in Hong Kong
6 4 2 5 3 1

To the Reader

In January 1848, James Marshall, who worked at Sutter's Mill in California, came upon some gold nuggets in the millstream. News of his discovery soon spread across the country, and the rush for gold began.

During the next fifty years or so, thousands of Americans streamed west. Some went to "hit it rich." Others went looking for a better way of life. They had heard that land was cheap and that crops grew in every season. For many, the American West became the promised land.

The Oregon Trail was one of the overland routes to the West. The trail followed old Indian paths that ran mostly along rivers. It was not really a road but merely ruts worn into the ground over the years by passing wagons. The trail left Missouri and followed the Platte River, cutting through what many called "oceans of grass." South Pass, Wyoming, marked the halfway point to California. From there, the trail wound through what one traveler called "a broken, rocky, and mountainous country." Beyond this was the desert and finally the Sierra Nevada Mountains. Another pioneer wrote that it was a "long and wearyful road, hot and dusty in summer; muddy, cold, and dreary in winter and fall."

The United States government encouraged pioneers to go west. People envisioned a nation stretching from the Atlantic to the Pacific. They called this expansion America's "manifest destiny."

This is the story of the Wards, an American family who followed the Oregon Trail to California in search of a better life. They packed up and left their home in Indiana to join a wagon train in 1853.

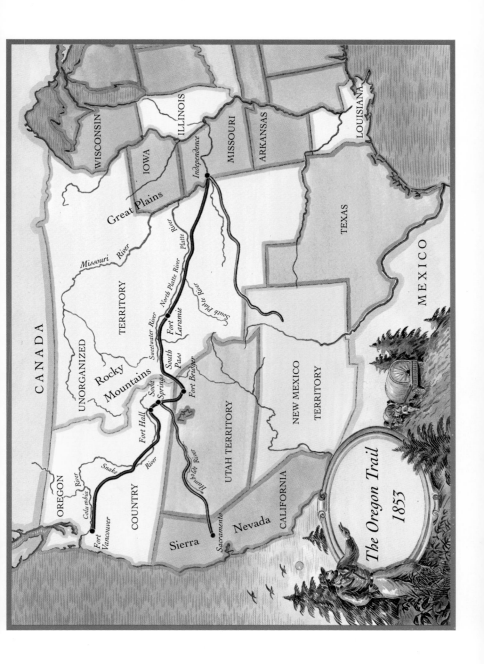

They swum the deep rivers and clumb the high peaks,
They rolled thro' the country for many long weeks,
Thro' all sorts of misery, dry days and wet,
If they hadn't gone on they'd be campin' there yet.
"Sweet Betsy from Pike," American folk song

*I*t was late afternoon of a brisk day in 1853.
A line of covered wagons moved slowly across
the plains of Kansas. The canvas covers of these
"prairie schooners" billowed in the wind, making them look at a distance like sailboats on a
sea of grass.

The air was heavy with dust, and a bank of
storm clouds formed on the horizon. The wagons, pulled by teams of oxen, swayed and rattled.
Women wearing sunbonnets and aprons walked
alongside, their children in hand. It was a great

A line of covered wagons moved slowly across the plains of Kansas.

relief to walk now and then and escape the constant jolting of the wagon. Sheep and goats trotted along trying to keep pace, and a cow tied to one of the wagons moved with difficulty. The men driving the wagons snapped their whips over the heads of the oxen. The wheels creaked and groaned as their speed increased. The wagon master galloped on horseback alongside

The wagon wheels creaked and groaned as their speed increased.

the wagon train, keeping a semblance of order.

"Another hour and we'll stop for the night!" he shouted.

In one wagon Harriet Ward tended her youngest child, Tommy, who was sick. She was traveling with her husband, James, and their three children. Ten-year-old Will was riding up front alongside his father. Francie, a pretty teenager with long brown braids, helped her mother tend to her little brother. She was placing a cool wet cloth on his fevered brow.

"I hope it's not cholera," Mrs. Ward said to Francie. News of an epidemic had reached their wagon train a few days before. Cholera was a constant concern. The crowded trail became a breeding ground for the highly infectious disease. Careless travelers left campsites littered with garbage and the foul bedding of those who had died from the disease. Infection was spread by flies and contaminated water. Cholera was never far away.

Up front, Mr. Ward tried to keep Will's spirits up. He painted a picture of how life would be when they reached the faraway land of

Francie helped her mother tend to her little brother.

California. "We'll eat from gold plates and have gold buttons on our shirts!" he told his son.

In early January, the Wards had first thought of immigrating to California. At the time, "gold fever" was rampant. Everywhere you went people were talking about gold in the West. Golden California was the answer to every problem. You could pick up enough gold in a single day to pay the debts of a lifetime. The California sunshine would cure all your ills. Fruits hung heavy on trees year-round. California was a dream come true!

The best oxen on the farm were selected to draw the Ward wagons. One wagon carried the family, and the other held their supplies. The supply wagon was filled with barrels of flour, beans, coffee, and dried meats. There was a gallon of wild plum preserves and several quarts of cherry jam. The wagon also held a supply of drinking water. The main wagon served as bedroom, sitting room, and kitchen. It carried trunks of clothing, a horsehair mattress, cooking utensils, books, and a medicine chest.

The supply wagon was filled with barrels of flour, beans, coffee,
and dried meats.

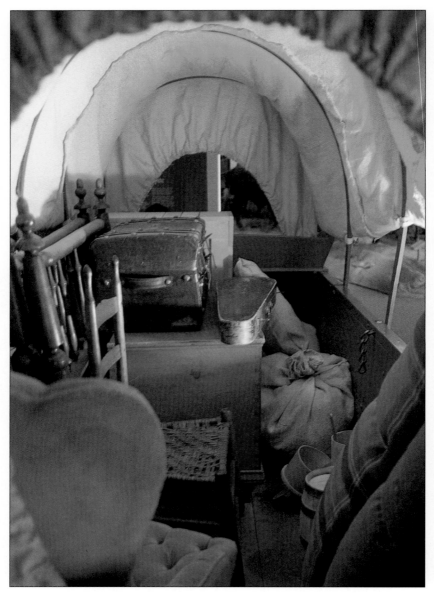

The main wagon served as bedroom, sitting room, and kitchen.

By 1849, an army of men, women, and children were heading for California and Oregon Country. There were several overland routes. The one the Wards traveled was the Oregon Trail. It started at Independence, Missouri, and ended, two thousand miles later, on the west coast. Twelve hundred miles into the journey, the trail split. Those headed for Oregon went right, and those headed for California turned left.

The people taking the overland routes faced a wilderness bigger than they had imagined. They put up with sizzling heat and bitter cold. They had no schools and no churches, nor doctors or hospitals. They had to depend on themselves and on one another. Many never made it.

"How do you feel, Tommy?" Mrs. Ward asked her son. She brushed some flies away from his face and placed another cloth on his head.

"I'm hot," he complained.

"I'll get my hat and fan him with it," Francie offered. She searched among some clothing and finally pulled out a wide-brimmed straw hat. While she fanned, the wagon hit a rut and heaved to one side.

"Take it easy!" Harriet Ward called out to her husband. "I've got a sick child back here!"

"Sorry, Mother," he answered, "but this trail is rough!"

There were two parts to a covered wagon, the box and the undercarriage. The box was the floor of the living and storage areas. The undercarriage held the wheels, axles, and steering mechanism. An oiled and waxed canvas cover stretched over the wagon bed on wooden hoops. This provided a waterproof shelter. Yet whenever it rained, water tended to leak in anyway.

The Wards' westward journey had begun months before. They had ridden a train, a wagon, and a river steamer to reach Independence. There they bought supplies and joined a wagon train. Founded in 1827, Independence had a reputation for being the best place for Oregon and California immigrants to buy their animals, wagons, and supplies. The town overflowed with wagonmakers, blacksmiths, gunsmiths, general stores, and livestock dealers. Oxen, horses, and mules could be had for a song.

By April, the Wards were ready to go. On the

sixteenth, their wagon and twenty others started off. Each day on the trip began early. The wagon master sounded a wake-up call on his bugle. Like a ship's captain, the wagon master was in command of the train. After a hurried breakfast, the travelers packed up their pots and pans, bedding and blankets. By daybreak they were on their way. In good weather the train could cover about fifteen miles a day. Inclement weather

After a hurried breakfast, the travelers packed up their pots and pans, bedding and blankets.

hampered their progress. The oxen were slow, but they were easy to handle and strong enough to pull the weight of a loaded wagon. And in an emergency they could be slaughtered and eaten as beef.

The days passed in much the same way. The wagon wheels creaked and shuddered across miles of rocky, rutted trail until around five in the afternoon. A site was chosen then by the wagon master, preferably near water. To make camp, one wagon turned to the right and the next to the left. In this way they formed a large circle. While the men and boys tended the animals and lit campfires within the circle, the women and girls prepared the evening meals. Some families pooled their provisions while others ate from their own store of food. Fuel for the campfires came from wood scraps and buffalo chips. Gathering the dried dung became a game for the children, with every child trying to find the biggest chip.

The evening meal was usually the same—bacon, beans, bread, and coffee. It was supplemented by wild berries or a rabbit, if the men

Fuel for the campfires came from wood scraps and buffalo chips.

were lucky enough to shoot one. Game was plentiful if you were not fussy. There was a ready supply of grouse, opossums, squirrels, wild turkeys, and prairie dogs. Of all the meats, the prairie dog, with its bitter taste, was liked the least.

Following the evening meal, the wagon master charted the next day's journey. He announced the route to the others and mentioned any places of interest along the way, such as settlements or military outposts.

Following the evening meal, the wagon master charted the next day's journey.

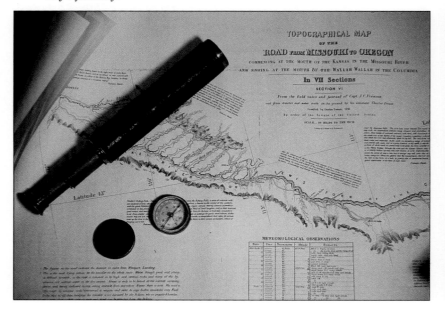

The men smoked their pipes and told stories from back home.

The men smoked their pipes and told stories from back home. Some made bets on the number of miles the wagons would cover the next day. The women sat together and chatted while knitting or mending clothing. Someone with a harmonica or banjo might play a familiar tune, prompting the group to sing along. The strains of "Home Sweet Home" or "My Old Kentucky Home" blended with the distant hooting of owls and the howling of coyotes. Lighthearted songs, such as "Ore-i-gon Boys," raised the spirits of the weary pioneers.

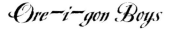

Ore-i-gon Boys

Come a-long, girls and lis-ten to my noise,

Don't you go and mar-ry no Ore-i-gon boys.

If you do your lot will be

John-ny-cakes and ven-i-son and sas-sa-fras tea,

John-ny-cakes and ven-i-son and sas-sa-fras tea.

When they come a-courting, I'll tell you what they wear:
An old leather coat all patched and bare,
An old straw hat more brim than crown,
And a pair of dirty socks they've worn the winter 'round. (2)

Someone with a harmonica or banjo might play a familiar tune.

When he comes in, first thing you hear,
"Madam, has your daddy killed a deer?"
And the next thing he says when he sits down,
"Madam, the johnnycake's too damn brown." (2)

Brandy is brandy any way you mix it,
An Ore-i-gon's an Ore-i-gon any way you fix it.
When other good folks have all gone to bed,
The Devil is a-working in the Ore-i-gon's head. (2)

For the children, it was early to bed. They slept huddled together on mats in the wagons, safe from the danger of wild animals. The adults slept on the ground near the campfires.

"How is Tommy?" one of the women asked Mrs. Ward before she retired for the night.

"I just put another wet cloth on his brow," she answered. "He will only take liquids. I gave him some molasses water this evening. He sipped on it and seemed to like it."

"That will keep his strength going," the woman told her, "but he needs an eggnog. If only we had some fresh eggs and milk."

"Too bad our cow is dry," another woman added.

"If we meet friendly Indians," the first woman said, "they might find us a few partridge eggs and some buffalo milk."

Most Native Americans were friendly and never bothered the wagon trains. But some resented the intrusion of the pioneers. These were a source of anxiety throughout the trip.

One night after midnight the wagon master shouted, "Indians! Indians!" The sleeping camp was thrown into confusion and great excitement. But the men responded. Each seized his gun and made ready for an attack. The women and children were instructed to seek shelter in the wagons and stay there. A few women screamed. Others followed their husbands. Several children jumped out of the wagons and started to cry. Then the wagon master announced that it was only a surprise drill. There was no real threat, but he wanted everyone to be prepared.

Harriet Ward was not amused.

"I have no need for surprises," she snapped at her husband. "Tommy is awake and most uncomfortable. If only I had some cool fresh water, I could bathe him and hope to break the fever."

It was always a happy time when the wagons camped near fresh water. A pond, stream, or river was always welcome. It provided water for washing and drinking. Water barrels were refilled, and everyone took a bath.

While traveling, the Ward children, with the exception of six-year-old Tommy, were drilled in

The sleeping camp was thrown into confusion and great excitement.

their lessons by their mother. She was determined not to neglect their schooling. They memorized grammar rules and history dates. Mrs. Ward held spelling bees and made up arithmetic rhymes, such as this one:

Twice two are four
Please shut the door.

Twice three are six
You're playing tricks.

Twice four are eight
Your hat's not straight.

Twice eleven are twenty-two
You forgot to tie your shoe.

Twice fifteen are thirty
My, your face is dirty.

Twice eighteen is thirty-six
Oil and water will not mix.

Years later, Will recalled the evening lessons: "Mother searched out her schoolbooks and turned a flour barrel into a desk. Children from other wagons often joined us when mother read poetry or told a story from history."

Her mother's efforts inspired Francie to dream of becoming a teacher. One evening after lessons, she told her mother, "I would like to teach school someday."

"You will need a good command of language," her mother replied. "You will need to read and write well and know your numbers." At the time, a person did not need a college diploma to teach school.

Mrs. Ward did not neglect her children's religious training either. She read to them from her Bible and taught them hymns. Strong religious convictions offered hope and guidance during a trip filled with hardship and danger.

Here and there along the Oregon Trail the pioneers came upon trading posts, military forts, and isolated farms. At the trading posts additional supplies could be bought and mail sent. Not all mail got through, and delivery was slow. But people could send a letter to family and

"Mother searched out her schoolbooks and turned a flour barrel into a desk."

friends back East, reporting on their progress. The United States Post Office Department had a difficult time handling the demand for mail service. Mail was carried by boat, horse, wagon, and stagecoach. It was frequently delayed or arrived smudged, torn, or mangled.

One morning in late June, the wagon train passed a farm. The house and barn sat on a grassy knoll on the shores of the Platte River. Mrs. Ward and some other women left the wagon train and called at the farmhouse.

"We need eggs and milk," one woman told the farmer's wife. "We have a sick child in need of solid nourishment."

"How long has the child been ailing?" the farmer's wife asked.

"About five weeks," Mrs. Ward told her. "He's good for a few days and then he fails. It's a strange sickness. I don't know what to do about it. And he has no appetite."

"It sounds like Rocky Mountain sickness," the farmer's wife speculated. "They say it comes from an insect bite."

She gave them six eggs and a pitcher of milk.

Using two of the eggs and some of the milk, Mrs. Ward made Tommy an eggnog. This is the way she made it:

Eggnog

1/2 cup sugar	4 cups of milk
3 tablespoons of sugar	1 teaspoon vanilla or
2 egg yolks	other flavoring
pinch of salt	2 egg whites

Beat the sugar into the egg yolks. Add a pinch of salt; stir into the milk. Cook, stirring constantly, over medium heat until the mixture coats a metal spoon. Add flavoring and cool.

Beat egg whites until foamy, gradually adding the three tablespoons of sugar. Beat into soft peaks. Add beaten whites to yolk mixture and blend well.

Tommy sipped the eggnog and seemed to enjoy it.

"I think I feel better," he told his mother. Mrs. Ward smiled and hoped it was true.

At the trading post in Fort Laramie, Mr. Ward bought a smoked ham. The Fourth of July was coming up, and he wanted his family to celebrate.

The wagon master announced that they would spend the holiday at Independence Rock. This smooth gray rock in central Wyoming was a half mile long and over a hundred feet high. It was named in honor of Independence Day, so it was a fitting place to celebrate the Fourth of July. Camp was made, and the holiday meal was prepared. Mrs. Ward cut thick slices of ham and served it with hot biscuits. She baked a pie using dried apples and raisins. Pioneer children poked fun at this simple pie in a silly rhyme:

Spit in my ear and tell me lies,
But don't feed me raisins and dry-apple pies!

After dinner that night it was proposed that everyone join in to celebrate the day. An American flag was found in one of the wagons and displayed in the center of the camp. Patriotic songs were sung, and one of the men recited the opening lines of the Declaration of Independence. Then the wagon master led the entire assembly in giving three cheers for the United States of America.

The men shot off their guns, and the women

The wagon master announced that they would spend the holiday at Independence Rock.

applauded. It was a wonderful celebration. Before leaving the rock, Will scratched all their names on its surface. This was a pioneer tradition. No one passed Independence Rock without leaving a mark.

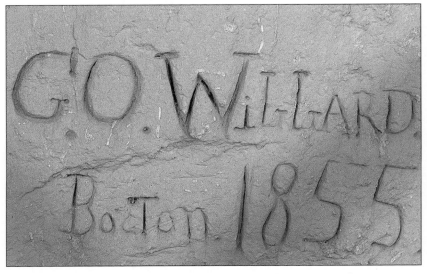

No one passed Independence Rock without leaving a mark.

"Did you put my name down?" Tommy asked his brother.

"Sure!" Will replied. "A hundred years from now, people will see your name and know that you were here!"

Pray that it is not his tombstone, Mrs. Ward said to herself. Her son's recovery was slow, and she was worried. He had lost weight and was pale and drawn.

All along the Oregon Trail were graves. Crude wooden crosses or scratched stones marked the resting places of those who had died along the way. Many were children. They were victims of disease and accidents. Lacking proper sanitation and a healthy diet, the pioneers were vulnerable to germs and malnutrition. Accidents were another hazard. On occasion, children fell from wagons and were crushed beneath the wheels. Cuts and wounds became infected and turned fatal.

Still another danger was crossing swollen rivers and streams. A rope was often stretched across the water to guide the wagons. Or the wagons were lifted off their wheels and floated across like rafts. Horses and cattle swam alongside. Both adults and children were known to drown.

On the twenty-third of August, 1853, the

Still another danger was crossing swollen rivers and streams.

wagon train arrived at Soda Springs in Idaho. Here the wagons separated. Those going to Oregon traveled northwest along the Snake River. Those heading for California went southwest. The parting at Soda Springs was always a sad time. Friendships formed along the way came to an end. There were tearful good-byes.

"I hope and pray that Tommy recovers," a friend told Harriet Ward. "If you could only get some medicine!"

"I doubt that we will find medicine until we arrive in California," Mrs. Ward answered.

The Wards watched as their friends departed.

The next morning the Wards' wagon and seven others started toward California. As the wagon master took his leave, he warned them to be on the lookout for armed bandits along the Humboldt River. He had heard that several of the wagons had been stripped of their possessions two weeks before. "Don't be tempted to take any shortcuts," the wagon master advised. "Stay on the established route. That's the safest!" They were on their way now, without an overseer to guide them.

By this time, Tommy was complaining of pains in his joints. He walked with difficulty and tossed and turned in his sleep.

"I think our boy is far sicker than we imagine," Mrs. Ward told her husband. "We should prepare the other children for the worst."

One evening after supper, she gathered Will and Francie around her and told them her greatest fear.

"Your little brother may die," she explained. "He is growing weaker every day. I want you to be prepared."

Francie started to cry, and Will tried to wipe away the tears filling his eyes.

"Is there nothing we can do for him?" Will questioned.

His mother shook her head. "Nothing but pray," she said quietly.

Within weeks, supplies ran short. There was just one sack of flour left, and the cornmeal and rice were gone. Meals were mostly soups made from greens picked along the way and thickened with a handful of flour. Mr. Ward told his children,

Now and then, bands of friendly Indians passed by.

"Watch what the animals eat. If they can eat it, it is likely we can, too."

Through Nevada, the wagons wound along two hundred miles of strange rock formations that rose from the flat, barren land. The only living things the travelers saw were insects and rattlesnakes. The heat was intense, and the landscape patched with dry grass and sagebrush. Nerves were taut, and throats were parched.

Cooking was done over sagebrush fires, and water was scarce. Now and then, bands of friendly Indians passed by and gave the travelers bear and deer meat.

On one such occasion, an Indian woman looked into the Wards' wagon and saw Tommy. By now he was painfully thin and asleep most of the time.

"Trouble?" the woman asked, using the few English words she knew. Mrs. Ward nodded her head. The woman crawled into the wagon and looked into Tommy's eyes. "I send medicine," the woman told her.

That same evening an Indian youth arrived

carrying a rawhide pouch. He handed it to Mrs. Ward and pointed toward the sick child. He indicated that she should mix the contents of the pouch with water and give it to Tommy. The pouch held a gray-green powder.

"We can't give it to him. We don't know what it is!" Mr. Ward objected.

"I don't care," his wife told him. "It is our only hope. He is growing weaker by the day. What else can we do?"

She mixed a little of the powder with water and gave it to her sick child. The next morning he seemed a little better. She continued the treatment. Within a week, color returned to his cheeks, and he was able to sit up.

"Is Tommy going to live?" Will asked.

"Let us hope and pray that he does," his mother replied.

By September the wagons reached the treacherous slopes of the Sierra Nevada. There were times when the wagons had to be hauled by rope up the mountains and the animals pushed

An Indian youth arrived carrying a
rawhide pouch.

and shoved along. Finally, one foggy morning they reached the summit of the peak. The fog swirled and then lifted. Bright sunshine burned away the mist. Through a clearing in the trees, they caught sight of the valley below.

"Look!" Harriet Ward called out. "It's California! That must be the Sacramento valley!" Below them lay the golden land they sought. She lifted Tommy out of the wagon so that he could see.

"We will celebrate Thanksgiving Day there," she promised. "We'll have meat and puddings and all the eggnog you can drink!"

Tommy smiled and hugged his mother.

"And I will find a school and be a teacher!" Francie added.

"And father will find gold and we'll all be rich!" Will shouted.

By the time the wagons had descended the mountains, Tommy was able to walk.

"It's a miracle!" Mr. Ward declared. "Whatever the Indian medicine was, it worked!"

"I will always be grateful to that Indian woman," Harriet Ward replied. "She saved our son's life."

The road to California ended in Sacramento. From here some of the wagon train went on to San Francisco and San Diego. The Wards stayed in Sacramento. Mr. Ward rented a small house for his family and went looking for gold. He found a few flakes, but that was all.

"My real fortune is having Tommy well and strong," he told his family.

Tommy's illness was most likely "mountain fever." This was a common ailment and was the collective name for several possible fevers. Some came from a tick-borne infection, and others were caused by contaminated drinking water. In any event, the Indian herbal medicine dispelled the fever, and Tommy's health improved.

As promised, the Ward family celebrated Thanksgiving Day in their new home. For dinner they had a grizzly bear steak, and Tommy enjoyed a frothy eggnog.

With little luck in his search for gold, Mr. Ward took a job in a lumber mill. Like many others who traveled west, he found not a land of "milk

Below them lay the golden land they sought.

and honey" but a life of hard work. A song of the period lamented:

> We found no gold but have to stay,
> We are too poor to get away.

There was no turning back. They had endured too much to get there. They had "swum the deep rivers and clumb the high peaks" and "rolled thro' the country for many long weeks." California had been their destination, and now it was their home.

Eventually Tommy and Will went to school, and Francie took a job as a clerk in a Sacramento dry goods store until she found a teaching position near Yuba City. Her hope to teach school came true.

Although the Ward family failed to strike it rich, they found more in California than a chance to dig for gold. They found a pleasant climate and an exciting alternative to the life they had left behind. Settled by a sudden rush of adventurers from all over the world, California was an exciting place to live. Foreign ideas, customs, and manners blended to make something altogether new. It was, as one visitor commented, "like a magic lantern show." The Wards were never sorry that they had cast their lot on the new frontier.

The Ward Family Tree

The grandfather of James Ward, the father in our story, was born in Ireland and migrated to Pennsylvania in the 1730s. His son John married Susanna Cummings in 1796. Their son James and his brother, Phillip, moved to Greene County, Indiana, around 1836.

The Wards of Oregon

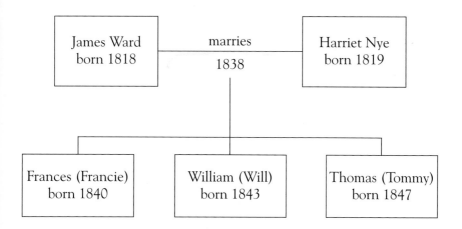

James Ward born 1818 — marries 1838 — Harriet Nye born 1819

Frances (Francie) born 1840

William (Will) born 1843

Thomas (Tommy) born 1847

Places to Visit

To learn more about the Oregon Trail, here are land-
marks and historic sites along the way:

Independence Square, Independence, Missouri
This is where the Oregon Trail began.

Scotts Bluff, Nebraska
A good source of trail lore, you will also find a
monument to the trail here.

Scotts Bluff

Independence Rock, Guernsey, Wyoming
This rock, on which pioneers scratched their
names, is called the "great register of the trail."

Fort Laramie National Park, U.S. Highway 26,
Wyoming
One of the major trading centers of the West and a
supply station for pioneers. Remains of twenty-one
historic buildings may be viewed. Operated by the
National Park Service.

South Pass City, twenty-six miles south of Lander,
Wyoming
A ghost town of the era. Here the Oregon Trail
passed the Continental Divide.

Jacksonville Historic District, Jacksonville, Oregon
Jacksonville was founded after a gold strike was
made nearby. Numerous commercial and residential
buildings remain, basically unaltered, making the
district an important example of a mid-nineteenth-
century western town.

Old Sacramento Historic District, Sacramento,
California
The original business district of Old Sacramento,
with a large number of buildings from the gold rush
period.

Books to Read

The following are books that will tell you more about the Oregon Trail:

Fiction

Chambers, Catherine E. *Wagons West: Off to Oregon.* Mahwah, NJ: Troll, 1984.

Kudlinski, Kathleen V. *Facing West: A Story of the Oregon Trail.* New York: Viking, 1994.

Nolan, Cecile. *A Journey West on the Oregon Trail.* Portland, OR: Rain Dance, 1993.

Van Leeuwen, Jean. *Bound for Oregon.* New York: Dial Books, 1994.

Nonfiction

Bird, Tia. *Dream Like Ezra: A Story of Pioneer Ezra Meeker.* Puyallup, WA: Kaleidoscope, 1994.

Fisher, Leonard E. *The Oregon Trail.* New York: Holiday House, 1990.

Hatch, Lynda. *The Oregon Trail.* Columbus, OH: Good Apple, 1994.

Stein, R. C. *The Story of the Oregon Trail.* Chicago: Children's Press, 1984.

Stickney, Joy. *Young Pioneers on the Oregon Trail.* Husum, WA: Canyon Creations, 1993.

Index

Page numbers for illustrations are in boldface.

About the Author

J. Loeper was born in Ashland, Pennsylvania. He has been a teacher, counselor, and school administrator. He has both taught and studied in Europe.

Mr. Loeper has contributed articles and poems to newspapers, journals, and national magazines. He is the author of more than a dozen books for young readers, all dealing with American history, and an active member of several historical societies. The *Chicago Sun* called him the "young reader's expert on Americana."

Mr. Loeper is also an exhibiting artist and has illustrated one of the books he authored. He and his wife divide their time between Connecticut and Florida.